Birming Tram

C000233958

on old picture postcards

John Marks

1. The site for the Moseley tram depot on the corner of Trafalgar Road was obtained in 1905. The large indicator board on the tram gives the destination as Moseley Road via Leopold Street, while the small blind announces it as Trafalgar Road. No indication of who published this c.1910 postcard.

**Printed by
Adlard Print and Typesetting Services,
Ruddington, Notts.**

£3.50

INTRODUCTION

This booklet is not intended to be a history of the tramway system in Birmingham and its suburbs, but to provide a nostalgic picture presentation. Those readers old enough to have travelled on them will remember the dangers of stepping off the pavement to board the tram in the middle of the road – something that would be even more hazardous today! As a young cyclist in those days, my other main memory is the danger of getting cycle wheels caught in the tram track. Another memory – one held in common with many thousands of other people – is rattling down the central reserve at great speed along Bristol Road on the way to the Lickeys: the journey was as much a part of the day's pleasure as the time spent on the hills.

The history of the Birmingham tramway system is quite complex since the North West of the city was connected with the many Black Country systems, while some areas now part of Birmingham were then independent authorities developing their own systems; there were also private interests. The acquisition of these interests and the development of the system is summarised in an excellent booklet *"A short review of Birmingham Corporation Tramways"* by P.L. Hardy and P. Jaques. I've attempted to show the differing forms of power: horse trams, steam trams, experiments with battery and cable cars with the final emergence of a unified overhead cable system. They became a memory on 4th July 1953 when buses took over the Short Heath, Pype Hayes and Erdington routes.

John Marks
March 1992

Picture Postcards were first published in Britain in 1894, but it was not until a decade later that they began to take off, when in 1902 the Post Office allowed a message to be written on the address side. This meant that the whole of one side was available for the picture and obviously gave more scope to publishers. Photographic viewcards became very popular, and the postcard became the most important way of communicating news or messages, in much the same way as the telephone is used today. The years up to 1914 were the 'Golden Age' of picture postcards, when millions of imaginative designs covering every subject under the sun were published by a host of national and local firms.

ISBN 0 946245 53 3

**Designed and published by
Reflections of a Bygone Age,
Keyworth, Nottingham 1992**
Reprinted 1997 and 2001

Front cover: Postcard published by Twilton Bros. featuring the first tramcar to arrive in Erdington on 1st March 1907. *(see also illus. 54)*

2. The Nechells horse trams were first operated on 11th November 1884 and replaced on 30th September 1906. They were followed by a temporary omnibus service while the line was electrified. This card was published by A. Twigg of 291 Bloomsbury Street.

3. Another view of the Nechells horse tram photographed by E. Ellis of 216 Bloomsbury Street. Horse-drawn vehicles differed from the electric trams in that they had two different-sized wheels on the outside.

4. Steam trams first ran in Birmingham in 1884. The Falcon engine and carriage seen here in Moat Row was photographed by Thos. Lewis of Stratford Road. The horse and cart in the foreground belonged to T. Harvey, coal dealer.

Alcester Road, Birmingham

Valentine's Series

5. There were seven steam tram routes; the one to Moseley Road was opened to Moseley in 1886 and on to Kings Heath in 1887. It was electrified in 1906. The horse and cart on this postcard by Valentine belonged to T.A. Law, another coal dealer.

6. The steam tram route to Perry Barr was opened on 25th November 1884. The terminus was in Birchfield Road, opposite the library. Aston Lane is in the middle distance. Postcard published by Scott Russell of Birmingham.

7. Steam trams in the Old Square, with Newbury's (later to become Lewis's) in the background. Postcard by Wrench of London about 1903.

In Remembrance of

SALTLEY, PERRY BARR, WITTON, & LOZELLS OLD STEAM TRAMS

WHICH STARTED
SERVICE
NOVEMBER 25th,
1884.

PASSING AWAY
OWING
TO AN ELECTRIC
SHOCK
JANUARY 1st, 1907.

"Let not ambition mock their useful toils,
Their homely joys and destiny obscure."

Photo by]   [P. King.

8. Steam trams last ran in Birmingham on 31st December 1906, and the event produced a number of commemorative cards like this. Some others had longer verses, and the general impression seemed to be that their passing was not a great loss.

9. Photographic postcard 'in memory of our old friend Saltley steam tram', published by A. Twigg.

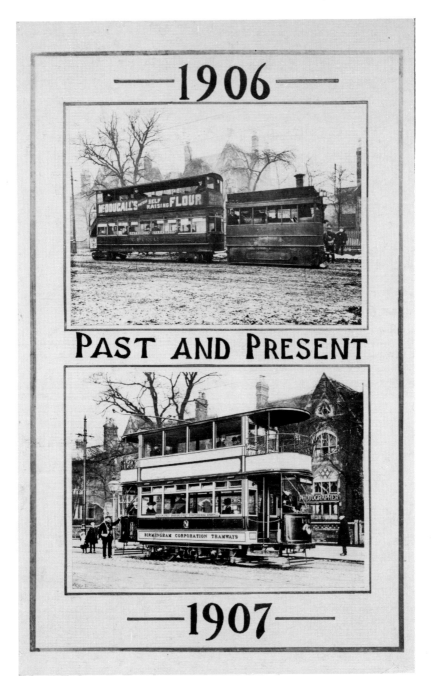

1906

PAST AND PRESENT

1907

10. Postcard publisher Thomas Lewis took these photos outside his premises on Stratford Road. Ironically, he died on a tram, tripping down the stairs of one in 1913 and fracturing his skull.

11. Battery or accumulator cars were experimented with on the Suffolk Street-Bristol Road route, firstly with a battery locomotive and carriage in 1888 and with the above self-contained unit in 1890. These lasted till May 1901 when the route was incorporated in the by now universally accepted overhead wire system.

12. Another experiment in electric traction was the cable car, where a cable in a central slot between the two lines was kept moving continually. The tram moved or stopped by attaching or detaching itself from the cable. This postcard by Knight Bros. shows a car in Colmore Row about 1906.

13. Cable car turning from Steelhouse Lane into Snow Hill, featured on a card by Wrench. In the background is the conventional overhead system.

14. Cable car in Soho Hill photographed by G.E. Lewis of 62 Station Street. The postcard was sent from Handsworth to Swansea in August 1911.

15. Cable car at the New Inns terminus. The system was opened from Colmore Row to Hockley Brook on 24th March 1888 and extended to the New Inns, Handsworth, in April 1889. When the line was electrified in 1911, it was extended to connect with West Bromwich at the 'Woodman' Inn. Wrench postcard, sent to France in June 1907.

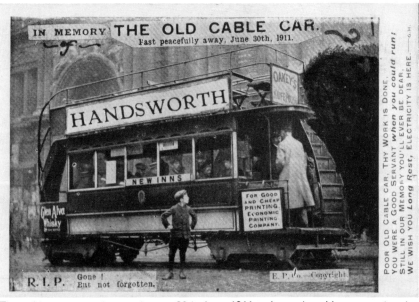

16. The cable car ceased operation on 30th June 1911 to be replaced by an overhead system. Postcard published by the Economic Printing Co. of 54 Pershore Street, Birmingham.

17. Electric tramcar no. 327 operating on Slade Road. The roller blind gives the route as Stockland Green to Steelhouse Lane. This was later numbered service no. 1. Postcard sent from Erdington in August 1915.

18. Stockland Green terminus, with single-decker no. 11 bus in the background. Postcard in 'Ana' series no. 316.

19. Six Ways, Aston, was on the route for a number of services with destinations in Erdington and Perry Barr.

20. High Street, Erdington, from the Gravelly Hill direction, with car no. 103 heading for Birmingham. Postcard postally used from Birmingham in September 1910.

21. Erdington tram terminus at Chester Road. This open top car has a roller blind destination. 1909 photographic postcard.

22. Another view of Erdington tram terminus on an anonymously-published postcard used from Haselor in June 1924. Car no. 694 has route no. 2 on the front. This route was closed on 5th July 1953.

23. Six Ways, Saltley, with tram no. 212 carrying the destination board Alum Rock Road to Martineau Street. Postcard by C.W. Selby of 434 Alum Rock Road. To the left of the picture is Gowan Road.

24. Looking the opposite direction from illus. 23, with tramcar no. 208 in view on a postcard sent from Birmingham in December 1910.

25. Service no. 6 from Martineau Street to Perry Barr. Car no. 11 is seen here in Corporation Street in 1935.

26. An open top car at Small Heath terminus by the park. Postcard used in July 1905.

27. Moseley Road, with car no. 137 stopped while two passengers have to walk to the middle of the road to get on – one of the dangers of tram travel! On the lamp-post is the small sign *"all cars stop here"*. The destination board displays Kings Heath via Bradford Street, together with a destination letter 'M'. The tram behind has 'B' for Balsall Heath. This photographic card dates from about 1910.

28. Car no. 337 on the Handsworth to Colmore Row route
the route split, one service carrying on to the city boun-
postcard of Soho Road, Handsworth, was published by J.

ndsworth, Birmingham

assengers by the old Council House. At Grove Road,
rvice 28), the other turning into Grove Road. This
n of Grimsby, and postally used in September 1914.

OXHILL ROAD, HANDSWORTH No 601.   COPYRIGH⏐ A

29. The service featured on illus. 28 next turned into Grove Road, carrying on to Oxhill Road, where car no. 326 is seen at the terminus. 'Adco' series postcard by Adams & Co. of Bristol Street, Birmingham.

30. A number of services ran from Edmund Street, branching off as the route ran towards the city boundary. Route 32 served Lodge Road and Winson Green, 31 Soho Station, 30 Cape Hill, and 29 Bearwood Road. There were also services to Oldbury and Dudley. Here car no. 29 is seen travelling along Dudley Road to Birmingham on a W.H. Day photographic postcard.

31. Car no. 27 on Dudley Road approaching Heath Green Road on a c.1910 postcard by Frank Nightingale of Smethwick.

32. The terminus of the Hagley Road (34) route at the 'King's Head' on the corner of Lordswood Road. Service no. 30, running along Dudley Road, did, however, follow Waterloo and Bearwood Roads to connect with Hagley Road. This postcard was used in June 1925.

33. Until 1910, the city boundary ran across Mary Street, hence the reason for a terminus at this point in Balsall Heath. In 1911 Moseley and Kings Heath were incorporated into Birmingham. Car no. 36 is seen here with the code 'B' for Balsall Heath.

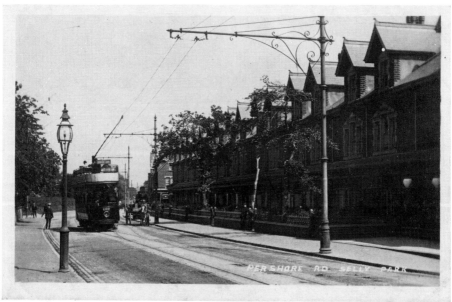

34. The Pershore Road route was originally built as single track with passing loops, and the tram here can be seen entering one such loop. The track was later relaid as double, except for one short length at Dogpool where, because of the narrowness of the road, a single track with one passing loop was retained until the closure of the line in 1952. Postcard used at Selly Oak in June 1917.

Stirchley

35. The interesting feature of this Stirchley card is the method of cleaning or repairing the standard carrying the overhead wires. The man with his ladder and handcart is working on a standard near Elm Tree Road. Postcard in Guest's series (no. 83), posted at Redditch in January 1907.

Stirchley

36. Car no. 242 opposite what is now Mayfield Road, Stirchley.

37. To the right of the tram is the entrance to the depot at Cotteridge, which was acquired from Kings Norton Council when it was incorporated in the city in 1911. The line was closed in 1952 and the site of the depot has been used for building houses. Card published by Edwards & Co. of New Street, mailed to Bournemouth in August 1911.

38. The tram depot at the corner of Moseley and Trafalgar Roads in 1906 on a postcard sent from Camp Hill in August 1908. Apparently because of the select residential area it then was, the depot was built to a more imposing design than others.

39. Though the lines in Moseley and Kings Heath were in Kings Norton and Northfield Urban District, they were operated by the City of Birmingham tramways department. The extension from Kings Heath to Alcester Lanes End was opened in January 1907. Edwards & Co. 'Clarence' series card no. 146.

40. Service no. 44 at Acocks Green terminus. The notice-board advertises a circular service via the Lickey Hills (adults 1/6, children 9d) and a special Sunday omnibus run at the same price. The 'New Inn' is in the background of this c.1930 postcard published by Wells' Library.

41. The Warwick Road tramway was opened in Broad Street in 1916 and to Weilley Road in 1922. This card of Acocks Green tram terminus is of particular interest as it shows the omnibus service 1A running from New Street to Moseley and Acocks Green.

42. The accumulator cars *(see illus. 11)* running on this route were replaced by overhead cables on 14th May 1901, and the route was extended to Selly Oak. 'Scott' series card no. 234.

43. The terminus at Selly Oak was opposite Chapel Lane at the 'Plough & Harrow'. This postcard, by Edwards & Co., posted on the morning of 6th August 1919 reads *"Tell Nellie shall not be back tonight"*, and was sent to Bordesley Green.

44. The central reservation tramway as far as Northfield was opened in 1923. Here, a service no. 70 is en route to Rednal. Many people will remember the excitement of travelling along this reservation where the trams seemed to reach colossal speeds. Postcard used from Birmingham in September 1927.

REDNAL, THE TRAM TERMINUS

45. The Northfield line was extended to Longbridge in December 1923 and to Rednal in April 1924. The terminus at that time was near Leach Green Lane. The final loop was completed in April 1925. Postcard published by B.J. Baker of Rednal Post Office.

Tram Terminus. Lickey, Rednal

46. Service no. 70 from Navigation Street to Rednal (8¼ miles) was the best-known in Birmingham, forming an integral part of a day out at the Lickeys. Waiting in the loop of the ornamental shelters was also part of the pleasure. Card published by Pinehurst Tea Gardens, Lickey Hills.

47. The last extension on this route was service no. 71 to Rubery, opened in February 1926. The tram terminus there is shown on a postcard sent to Leamington Spa in July 1931. *"Enjoyed my few days, feel all the better for a rest, lovely scenery"*, wrote Ida.

48. Laying track and installation of the overhead equipment caused considerable disruption to other traffic, as can be judged from this view of work being carried out at Six Ways Junction, Aston Manor, probably in 1906.

49. A fine close-up of car 104. The side destination board reads Navigation Street, Hurst Street, Balsall Heath, Cannon Hill Park, while the front board advertises Cannon Hill Park to Navigation Street, along with the letter 'C' for Cannon Hill. To the right of the tram can be seen the time clock found at all termini. Anonymously-published c.1912 postcard.

50. The elaborate cast iron and glass shelters at Dale End partially obscure car 203 picking up passengers. The end of the shelter reads *"Cars load here for Small Heath, Coventry Road and Hay Mills – Warwick Road & Acocks Green, Stratford Road and St. Johns Road – Moseley Road, Kings Heath and Alcester Lane End."*

51. Trams were frequently decorated and illuminated for special events, and it must have been a wonderful sight. It was recorded that 5,000 lamps and a mile of wire were required to produce the right effect on this tram, decorated for George V's coronation in June 1911.

52. This car was decorated to commemorate the visit of King Edward VII and Queen Alexandra to open Birmingham University on 7th July 1909. It was photographed in the same depot as the tram in illus. 51, and the card was published by Stanford & Mann.

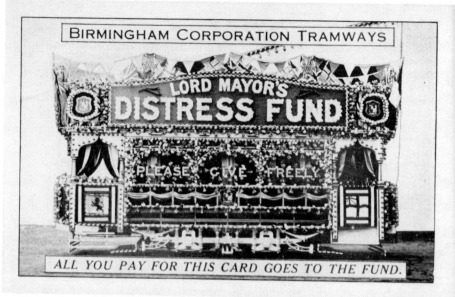

BIRMINGHAM CORPORATION TRAMWAYS

LORD MAYOR'S DISTRESS FUND

PLEASE GIVE FREELY

ALL YOU PAY FOR THIS CARD GOES TO THE FUND.

53. Another special car, this time for the 'Lord Mayor's Distress Fund', presumably during World War I.

ERDINGTON TRAMS, FIRST CAR.
Photographed at Terminus, Sutton Road, March 1st, 1907
Twilton Bros., Publishers, Erdington

54. A postcard published by Twilton Bros. of 87 High St., Erdington to commemorate the opening of the Erdington tramway service on 1st March 1907. Compare the card on the front cover.

FATAL TRAM ACCIDENT IN
WARSTONE LANE.

55. This accident in Warstone Lane resulted in nineteen people being injured, two of them fatally. There was much correspondence in the local newspapers about excessive speeds, though the accident – on 1st October 1907 – was due to brake failure. This card, published by Scott Russell & Co., was posted from Birmingham two days after the crash.

Fatal Tram Accident in Birmingham, October 1st, 1907:— 2 KILLED, 17 INJURED.
EDWARDS & CO., Publishers, B'ham.   A. DARK, Printer, 358, Stratford Rd., B'ham.

56. This view by Edwards & Co. shows the tram being lifted. On the left can be seen the heavy wooden structure that had to be built before this could be carried out.

57. The staff of the tramways department had an annual parade and church service. They gathered in Great Charles Street or Colmore Row, were inspected by the Lord Mayor and then marched to St. Martin's. This card shows the Mayor inspecting tramways staff on 1st June 1911 in Colmore Row. It was posted to Liverpool a month later

58. Another church parade, this time on 31st May 1908, photographed by E.F.S. Dolby.

59. The message on this card reads "This church parade took place on Sunday 8 a.m. and then we marched to St. Martin's for the 9 a.m. service." The photograph was taken at the top end of Great Charles Street, and the card was posted to Acocks Green on 2nd June 1912.